CHRISTMAS AT HOME
Delightful Desserts

Compiled by Emily Biggers.

ISBN 978-1-60260-971-6

All scripture quotations are taken from the King James Version of the Bible.

Published by Barbour Publishing, Inc., P.O. Box 719, Uhrichsville, Ohio 44683, www.barbourbooks.com

Our mission is to publish and distribute inspirational products offering exceptional value and biblical encouragement to the masses.

Member of the
Evangelical Christian
Publishers Association

Printed in China.

CHRISTMAS AT HOME
Delightful Desserts

BARBOUR
PUBLISHING

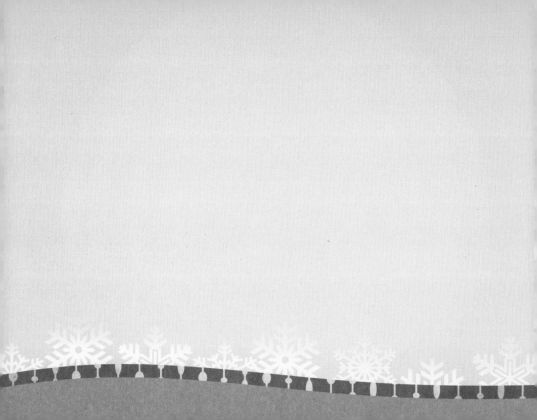

CONTENTS

WARM UPS: HOLIDAY BEVERAGES

Christmas is not just a day, an event to be observed and speedily forgotten. It is a spirit which should permeate every part of our lives.

WILLIAM PARKS

HOLIDAY HOT CHOCOLATE MIX

2 cups nonfat dry milk powder
¾ cup sugar
½ cup unsweetened cocoa

½ cup mini semisweet chocolate chips
½ cup powdered nondairy creamer
⅛ teaspoon salt

Use a whisk to blend all ingredients evenly in a bowl. Store mix in an airtight container at room temperature. To serve: Put 3 to 4 generous tablespoons of hot chocolate mix into mug. Add boiling water. Stir well. Top with whipped cream or mini marshmallows. Yield: about 4 cups hot chocolate mix

Variations:
Substitute powdered sugar for sugar.
Add crushed peppermint or crème de menthe candies, white chocolate chips, or toffee bits. Use flavored powdered creamers.

HOT APPLE CIDER

7 cups apple cider
2 cups orange juice
½ cup honey
3 whole cloves
1 apple, peeled
1 orange, peeled and sliced

Combine cider, orange juice, and honey in a Dutch oven. Insert cloves into apple. Add apple and orange slices to juice mixture, and bring to a boil. Reduce heat and simmer 15 minutes. Remove from heat, and let stand about 5 minutes. Yield: 2 quarts

HOT SPICED TEA

1 large package unsweetened lemonade mix
¾ cup unsweetened instant tea mix
2 cups sugar
1½ cups orange-flavored drink mix
2 teaspoons ground cinnamon
1 teaspoon ground cloves

Blend all ingredients thoroughly in large mixing bowl, and then store in covered jar or airtight container. Mix 2 level teaspoons per 1 cup hot water for hot spiced tea.

EASY SPARKLING CRANBERRY PUNCH

64 ounces cranberry-apple juice, chilled
1 (2 liter) bottle ginger ale, chilled

In a punch bowl, combine juice and ginger ale. Serve chilled.

HOLIDAY MOCHA PUNCH

6 cups water
½ cup instant chocolate drink mix
½ cup sugar
1 to 2 tablespoons instant coffee granules
½ gallon vanilla ice cream
½ gallon chocolate ice cream
Whipped cream (optional)
Chocolate curls (optional)

In a large saucepan, bring water to a boil. Remove from heat. Add chocolate drink mix, sugar, and coffee; stir until dissolved. Place mixture in pitcher, cover, and refrigerate at least 4 hours or overnight. About 30 minutes before serving, pour mixture into a large punch bowl. Add vanilla and chocolate ice cream by scoopfuls; stir until partially melted. Garnish with dollops of whipped cream or chocolate curls if desired. Yield: 20 to 25 servings (about 5 quarts)

MOM'S STOVETOP HOT COCOA

6 tablespoons baking cocoa
6 tablespoons sugar
Dash salt
⅓ cup water
6 cups milk
1 teaspoon vanilla
Whipped cream (optional)
Nutmeg (optional)
Candy canes (optional)

In medium saucepan, dissolve cocoa, sugar, salt, and vanilla in water. Boil gently over low heat for 2 minutes, stirring. Add milk; heat thoroughly, but do not boil. Just before serving, beat with mixing spoon or hand beater until smooth and foamy; add vanilla. After pouring into cups, add whipped cream if desired and dust with nutmeg. In each cup, place a candy cane for stirring. Yield: 6 to 8 servings

PEPPERMINT COCOA IN A JAR

½ cup powdered coffee creamer
1 (2.25 ounce) bottle red sugar
¼ cup peppermint candies, finely crushed
1 circle waxed paper
⅓ cup powdered sugar
½ cup dry chocolate milk mix
½ cup dry milk

Place ingredients in a pint-size jar in the order above, starting with the coffee creamer and ending with the dry milk. The paper circle should be placed between crushed mint layer and powdered sugar layer to keep sugar from shifting down through mints. Decorate jar as desired. Attach directions on next page to the jar.

Note: If you are not making this as a layered jar gift, you may wish to simply blend all the ingredients together with a whisk or spoon in a large mixing bowl and then store in a jar or an airtight container.

Directions:
Empty cocoa mix into a bowl. Remove and discard paper circle. Blend the mix together with a whisk. Place mix back into jar. Place 1½ to 2 tablespoons cocoa mix into cup. Add 1 cup boiling water. Stir until dissolved. Top with whipped cream and sprinkle lightly with red sugar crystals if desired.

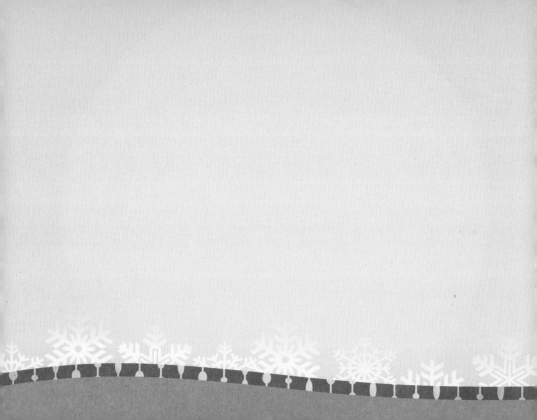

12 DAYS OF CHRISTMAS: BREAKFAST SWEETS

Now when Jesus was born in Bethlehem of Judaea in the days of Herod the king, behold, there came wise men from the east to Jerusalem, saying, Where is he that is born King of the Jews? For we have seen his star in the east, and are come to worship him.

Matthew 2:1–2

CRANBERRY-ORANGE CHRISTMAS TART

1 cup butter or margarine
1 cup sugar
3 egg yolks
1 cup toasted, finely chopped hazelnuts
1¼ cups flour
½ teaspoon salt, divided
3 cups fresh cranberries
½ cup light brown sugar, firmly packed
3 to 4 tablespoons grated orange zest
⅓ cup orange juice
Whole hazelnuts
Whipped cream

Cream butter and sugar until light and fluffy. Stir in egg yolks, chopped nuts, flour and ¼ teaspoon salt. Mix well. Chill dough about 1½ hours or until firm enough to handle. Combine cranberries, brown sugar, orange zest, orange juice, and remaining salt in medium saucepan. Bring to a boil. Simmer uncovered 10 to 15 minutes or until mixture is as thick as jam. Cool. Set aside about ⅓ cup dough. Press remaining dough against bottom and sides of 9½-inch tart or cake pan. Spread cranberry mixture over dough in pan. Roll out reserved dough on floured surface to ¼-inch thickness. Cut into strips. Arrange in a lattice pattern on top of cranberry mixture. Place a whole hazelnut in each square of lattice. Bake at 375 degrees for 35 to 40 minutes or until brown. Serve with whipped cream.

JELLY ROLL

1 cup sifted cake flour
1 teaspoon baking powder
¼ teaspoon salt
4 eggs
½ teaspoon lemon extract
1 teaspoon vanilla

1 cup sugar
⅓ cup hot water
2 tablespoons butter, melted
1 cup jelly or jam (plum, apricot,
    peach, etc.)
Powdered sugar

Line bottom of 13x10x1-inch jelly roll pan with waxed paper. Preheat oven to 400 degrees. Sift together flour, baking powder, and salt. Beat eggs and flavorings in large mixing bowl on high speed for 1 minute. Continue beating while adding sugar slowly. Beat until very thick (about 2½ minutes). Combine hot water and butter; add to flour mixture. Beat on medium-low speed just until blended (about 1 minute). Remove from mixer; fold over and over with spatula a few times. Turn into pan, spreading evenly. Bake 15 to 18 minutes, or until light brown. Lay a clean dish towel on flat surface and dust lightly with powdered sugar. Take cake from oven and loosen sides with a spatula. Invert on the dish towel. Carefully peel off the paper and quickly trim edges smoothly all around cake. Roll up cake loosely, rolling towel with it. Cool about 10 minutes, then unroll, leaving on the towel. Spread all over with jelly to within ½ inch of edges. Roll up, lifting off towel in the process. Tuck open end under. Cool. Sift powdered sugar on top.

CINNAMON ROLLS NOEL

2 cups flour
2 teaspoons baking powder
½ teaspoon salt
5 tablespoons butter, divided
⅔ cup milk
⅓ cup sugar
½ teaspoon cinnamon

Glaze:
1½ tablespoons butter or margarine,
  softened
1 cup sifted powdered sugar
1 tablespoon milk

Stir flour, baking powder, and salt together. Cut in 4 tablespoons butter. Add milk gradually until soft dough is formed. On slightly floured board, roll the dough flat to ¼-inch thickness Cream 1 tablespoon butter, sugar, and cinnamon. Spread mixture over dough. Starting from one edge, roll dough, forming a long roll. Cut roll into eight 1-inch slices. Place slices on a cookie sheet. Bake at 425 degrees for 15 minutes. Turn heat down to 350 degrees and bake 15 minutes longer. Cool slightly. Meanwhile, for the glaze, beat butter at medium speed with electric mixer. Add powdered sugar and milk, beating until blended. Spread over cooled rolls. Yield: 8 rolls

ORANGE-PECAN WAFFLES

⅔ cup butter or margarine
3 cups sifted flour
3 teaspoons baking powder
1 teaspoon salt
2 tablespoons sugar

4 large eggs
2¼ cups milk
1½ teaspoons vanilla
Zest of 1 orange
1 cup pecans, finely chopped

Melt and cool butter. Set aside. Sift flour, baking powder, salt, and sugar together in large bowl. Beat eggs in small bowl on high speed for 1 minute. Add milk and vanilla. Then add egg mixture to dry ingredients. Add orange zest and pecans. Beat on medium speed about 1 minute until blended. Blend in butter on low speed. Bake in preheated waffle maker. Makes 4 full-size, four-section waffles. Serve with additional butter and warm maple syrup.

CHRISTMAS MORNING CAKE

¼ cup sugar
¼ cup pecans, chopped
2 teaspoons cinnamon
½ cup butter, softened
⅓ cup pecans, chopped
1 box yellow cake mix
1 (3¼ ounce) box vanilla instant
  pudding
¾ cup cooking oil
¾ cup water
4 eggs
1 teaspoon vanilla

Glaze:
1 cup sifted powdered sugar
3 tablespoons milk
½ teaspoon vanilla
½ teaspoon butter extract

Mix together sugar, ¼ cup chopped pecans, and cinnamon; set aside. Grease Bundt pan with butter, and sprinkle ⅓ cup chopped pecans to cover bottom. In medium bowl with electric mixer, combine cake mix, pudding, oil, and water. Add eggs, 1 at a time, and beat 6 minutes. Mix in vanilla. Alternate layering batter and cinnamon mixture in Bundt pan, beginning and ending with the batter. Bake at 350 degrees for 40 to 50 minutes, until toothpick inserted near center of cake comes out clean. Cool on rack for 8 minutes. Remove cake from pan and place on plate.

While cake is cooling, prepare glaze by mixing together all ingredients until well-blended. Pour glaze over warm cake.

LISA'S POPPY SEED COFFEE CAKE

1 cup cooking oil
4 eggs
1 cup hot water
1 box butter pecan cake mix
1 (3¼ ounce) box toasted coconut instant pudding
¼ cup poppy seeds

Combine all ingredients. Lightly spray 2 loaf pans with cooking spray. Divide batter evenly between loaf pans. Bake at 325 degrees 40 to 45 minutes. Cool 5 to 10 minutes in pans. Then turn out on a rack to cool. Serve with butter.

MARTHA'S BLUEBERRY BREAK MUFFINS

1 cup fresh or frozen blueberries
2 tablespoons butter
1 cup sugar
2 eggs
2 cups flour
2½ teaspoons baking powder
¾ cup milk

Wash blueberries, drain thoroughly, and set aside. Cream butter and sugar together. Mix in eggs, flour, and baking powder. Add milk, and beat. This will make a stiff dough. Carefully fold in blueberries. Bake in well-greased muffin tins at 350 degrees for 25 to 30 minutes. Yield: 12 muffins

HOLIDAY PUMPKIN MUFFINS

2¼ cups baking mix
½ cup plus 2 tablespoons sugar substitute
2 teaspoons pumpkin pie spice
¼ cup pecans, chopped
2 eggs, slightly beaten
2 cups pumpkin puree
¼ cup sour cream
½ cup cream cheese, softened

Preheat oven to 375 degrees. Spray muffin pans with cooking spray or line with paper liners. In a large bowl, combine baking mix, ½ cup sugar substitute, pumpkin pie spice, and pecans. Add eggs, pumpkin, and sour cream. Mix well to combine. Fill 12 prepared muffin wells ⅓ full. In a small bowl, stir cream cheese with a spoon until softened. Serve muffins warm with cream cheese for spreading. Yield: 12 muffins

FESTIVE FRENCH TOAST

2 eggs
¼ teaspoon salt
1 tablespoon sugar
¼ cup light or heavy cream
2 teaspoons vanilla
Butter or margarine
6 white or whole wheat bread slices

Separate eggs. Beat egg whites with salt and sugar until stiff. Beat yolks until thick and lemon-colored; add cream and vanilla. Fold egg white mixture into yolk mixture. Quickly dip bread slices, one at a time, into egg mixture; turn until just well-coated, not soggy. In hot butter, brown at once on both sides. Serve immediately with butter, syrup, and/or powdered sugar. Yield: 6 servings

FLUFFY GRIDDLE CAKES

2 cups flour
3 teaspoons baking powder
1 teaspoon salt
2 tablespoons sugar
1 egg
1½ cups milk
3 tablespoons cooking oil

Sift flour, baking powder, salt, and sugar into large mixing bowl. In a separate bowl, beat egg well and add milk. Pour egg mixture over dry ingredients and beat on medium speed with mixer until blended (about 1 minute). Quickly blend in oil. Bake on preheated griddle, turning only once to brown on both sides. Yield: about 2 dozen pancakes

MOM'S BANANA NUT BREAD

3 large ripe bananas
1 cup sugar
1 egg, slightly beaten
1½ cups flour
¼ cup margarine, melted
1 teaspoon salt
1 teaspoon baking soda
¼ cup buttermilk
½ cup pecans, chopped

Mash bananas in large mixing bowl. Stir in remaining ingredients and blend well. Bake at 325 degrees for 1 hour in a greased and floured loaf pan. Cool slightly and turn out on plate for serving. Serve warm with butter.

CRANBERRY-ORANGE BREAD

2 cups flour
1½ teaspoons baking powder
½ teaspoon baking soda
½ teaspoon salt
2 tablespoons shortening
¾ cup orange juice
1 egg, beaten
1 tablespoon grated orange zest
½ teaspoon vanilla (or almond) extract
1½ cups cranberries, coarsely chopped

Mix all ingredients together throughly. Bake in large greased and floured loaf pan at 350 degress for 1 hour.

SANTA'S DREAM: COOKIES, BROWNIES & BARS

I truly believe that if we keep telling the Christmas story, singing the Christmas songs, and living the Christmas spirit, we can bring joy and happiness and peace to this world.

NORMAN VINCENT PEALE

CANDY CANE COOKIES

1 cup shortening, softened
1 cup powdered sugar
1 egg
1½ teaspoons peppermint extract
1 teaspoon vanilla
2½ cups flour
½ teaspoon salt
½ teaspoon red food coloring
Sugar

Preheat oven to 375 degrees. Mix shortening, powdered sugar, egg, and flavoring extracts. Add flour and salt, and blend together. Divide dough in half. Add red food coloring to half of dough. Roll a 4-inch strip from each half of divided dough. Twist together and shape like a candy cane. Sprinkle with sugar. Bake at 375 degrees for 10 minutes on ungreased baking sheet.

EGGNOG COOKIES

1 cup butter or margarine, softened
2 cups sugar
1 cup eggnog
1 teaspoon baking soda
½ teaspoon nutmeg
5½ cups flour

Frosting:
3 cups powdered sugar
¼ cup butter or margarine, softened
⅓ cup eggnog

Beat butter and sugar until fluffy. Add eggnog, baking soda, and nutmeg; mix well. Gradually add flour, mixing well. Divide dough in half; wrap in plastic. Chill overnight in refrigerator or 2 hours in freezer. On floured surface, roll out half of dough to ⅛-inch thickness. Cut out with flour-dipped Christmas cookie cutters. Place 1 inch apart on ungreased baking sheet. Bake at 375 degrees for 8 to 10 minutes, or until lightly browned. Cool completely.

Frosting: Beat powdered sugar and butter until well blended. Gradually beat in eggnog until icing is smooth. Spread on cooled cookies.

GINGER CREAM COOKIES

½ cup shortening
1 cup sugar
2 eggs
1 cup molasses
4 cups flour
1 teaspoon salt

2 teaspoons ginger
1 teaspoon ground cloves
1 teaspoon cinnamon
2 teaspoons baking soda
1 cup hot water

Cream shortening, sugar, and eggs. Add molasses. Sift together all dry ingredients, except baking soda. Dissolve baking soda in hot water; add alternately to dry ingredients. Chill dough thoroughly. Drop by teaspoonfuls 2 inches apart onto greased cookie sheets. Bake at 400 degrees for 8 minutes. While still warm, ice with a thin white frosting of your choice.

QUICK & EASY PEANUT BUTTER COOKIES

1 cup peanut butter
1 egg
1 cup sugar

Spray two cookie sheets with vegetable cooking spray. Mix ingredients together and drop by spoonfuls onto cookie sheets. Bake at 350 degrees for 8 to 12 minutes. Do not brown cookies on top as bottoms will burn. Yield: 3 dozen

GINGERBREAD BOYS

¼ cup brown sugar
½ cup butter
2 medium eggs
¼ cup molasses
3¼ cups flour
¾ teaspoon ginger

1½ teaspoons baking soda
½ teaspoon cinnamon
½ teaspoon nutmeg
½ teaspoon salt
Gingerbread boy cookie cutter

Beat sugar and butter until well blended. Add eggs and molasses. Stir in remaining ingredients. Cover; chill 1 hour. Roll out to about ¼-inch thickness and cut out gingerbread boys. Bake at 350 degrees for 10 minutes. When cool, make powdered sugar icing or use purchased prepared vanilla icing to decorate. Note: Candy-coated chocolate candies may also be used to decorate cookies before baking.

STIR & DROP SUGAR COOKIES

2 eggs
⅔ cup vegetable oil
2 teaspoons vanilla
1 teaspoon lemon zest
¾ cup sugar
2 teaspoons baking powder
2 cups flour
½ teaspoon salt
Vegetable oil
Sugar

Beat eggs; stir in oil, vanilla, and lemon zest. Blend in sugar and beat until thick. Add remaining ingredients. Drop 2 inches apart onto ungreased cookie sheets. Flatten with glass dipped in oil and sugar. Bake at 400 degrees 8 to 10 minutes.

CHRISTMAS SUGAR COOKIES

4 cups sifted cake flour
2½ teaspoons baking powder
½ teaspoon salt
⅔ cup shortening, softened
1½ cups sugar
2 eggs
1 teaspoon vanilla or peppermint extract
4 teaspoons milk

Sift flour, baking powder, and salt and set aside. In large mixing bowl, mix shortening with sugar, eggs, and flavoring until very light and fluffy. Add flour mixture and milk alternately. Wrap cookie dough in waxed paper and chill for several hours or overnight. (This process may be shortened by placing cookie dough in freezer for approximately 30 minutes.) Heat oven to 375 degrees. Separate chilled cookie dough into halves or thirds. On lightly floured surface, roll a portion of the dough about ¼-inch thick.

With floured Christmas cookie cutters, cut dough into desired shapes. Arrange cookies ½ inch apart on lightly greased cookie sheet. Brush cookies lightly with milk or with egg white diluted with 1 teaspoon water. Then sprinkle cookies with red and green sugar. Bake at 375 degrees for 8 to 10 minutes or until delicately browned. Cool. Yield: 5 to 6 dozen cookies

MERRY CHRISTMAS SUGAR COOKIES

1 cup butter, softened
1½ cups powdered sugar
1 teaspoon vanilla
1½ teaspoons almond extract
1 teaspoon cream of tartar
1 teaspoon baking soda
1 egg
2½ cups flour
Red and green icing and/or sugar (optional)
Mini cinnamon candies or candy-coated chocolate candies (optional)

Mix together first 8 ingredients to form dough. Wrap dough thoroughly in waxed paper and chill about 2 hours. Roll out dough and cut out cookies with cookie cutters. Bake at 375 degrees for 7 to 8 minutes. Do not overbake. Cool. Frost cookies with a basic powdered sugar icing recipe and sprinkle with red and/or green sugar. Top with miniature cinnamon candies or candy-coated chocolate candies.

SECRET KISS COOKIES

1 cup butter, softened
½ cup sugar
1 teaspoon vanilla
1¾ cups flour
1 cup walnuts, finely chopped
1 (6 ounce) bag chocolate kiss candies
Powdered sugar

Beat butter, sugar, and vanilla until light and fluffy. Add flour and walnuts; mix well. Chill dough for 1 to 2 hours. Remove wrappers from chocolate kisses. Shape about 1 tablespoon dough around each chocolate kiss. Roll to make ball. (Be sure to cover chocolate completely.) Bake at 375 degrees for 10 to 12 minutes. While still slightly warm, roll in powdered sugar.

BURIED CHERRY COOKIES

1 cup sugar
½ cup margarine
1 egg
1½ teaspoons vanilla
1½ cups flour
⅓ cup baking cocoa
¼ teaspoon baking powder

¼ teaspoon baking soda
¼ teaspoon salt
1 (6 ounce) jar maraschino cherries,
   drained well, juice reserved
½ cup semisweet chocolate chips
¼ cup sweetened condensed milk
2 teaspoons cherry juice

Cream sugar and margarine. Beat in egg and vanilla. Add flour, cocoa, baking powder, baking soda, and salt; mix. Shape dough into 1-inch balls. Press down center with thumb and put a cherry in the indentation. In a double boiler, melt together chocolate chips, condensed milk, and cherry juice. Cover cookies with this "frosting." Bake at 350 degrees for 8 to 10 minutes.

CINNAMON TWISTIES

2 cups sugar
2 cups walnuts, ground
1 tablespoon cinnamon
1 cup butter, softened
1 (8 ounce) package cream cheese, softened
2½ cups flour
1 egg, beaten

Mix together sugar, walnuts, and cinnamon; set aside. In another bowl, cream butter and cream cheese. Gradually add flour. If dough is too soft, add a little more flour. Roll out dough to ½-inch thickness and brush with beaten egg. Cover with cinnamon mixture. Cut into 1½-inch strips and twist. Place on ungreased cookie sheets. Bake at 400 degrees for 8 to 10 minutes.

CHOCOLATE SNOWBALLS

1¼ cups butter, softened
⅔ cup sugar
1 teaspoon vanilla
2 cups flour
⅛ teaspoon salt
½ cup baking cocoa
2 cups pecans, chopped
½ cup powdered sugar

In medium bowl, cream butter and sugar until light and fluffy. Stir in vanilla. Sift together flour, salt, and cocoa; stir into creamed mixture. Mix in pecans until well blended. Cover and chill for at least 2 hours. Preheat oven to 350 degrees. Roll chilled dough into 1-inch balls. Place about 2 inches apart on ungreased cookie sheets. Bake 20 minutes in preheated oven. Roll in powdered sugar when cooled.

GINGERSNAPS

2 cups flour
2 teaspoons baking soda
¼ teaspoon salt
1 teaspoon cinnamon
1 teaspoon ground cloves
1 teaspoon ground ginger

¾ cup butter or margarine, softened
1 cup sugar
1 egg
¼ cup molasses
Additional sugar

In a small bowl, sift together flour, baking soda, salt, cinnamon, cloves, and ginger. Set aside. In a mixing bowl, cream together butter and sugar. Add egg and molasses and beat well. Gradually mix in dry ingredients. Mix well. Chill dough for 1 to 2 hours. Form dough into 1-inch balls and roll in additional sugar. Place balls 2 inches apart on ungreased cookie sheets. Bake at 375 degrees for 10 minutes or until cookies are set and tops begin to crack. Cool on wire racks. Yield: 4 dozen cookies

PUMPKIN DIP

2 cups canned pumpkin
3 cups powdered sugar
2 (8 ounce) packages cream cheese, softened
2 tablespoons cinnamon

Blend all ingredients. Serve with gingersnaps.

LEMON WAFERS

½ cup butter, softened
½ cup sugar
2 large eggs, lightly beaten
1 teaspoon vanilla
Zest of 2 lemons
1 teaspoon lemon juice
1¼ cups sifted flour
⅛ teaspoon salt

Cream butter and sugar in a large bowl until light and fluffy. Add eggs, vanilla, lemon zest, and lemon juice; mix well. Fold in flour and salt. Chill for at least 1 hour. Heat oven to 350 degrees. Lightly grease cookie sheets. Drop dough by teaspoonfuls about 1½ inches apart onto prepared cookie sheets. Bake 6 to 7 minutes, until edges are very lightly browned. Cool on pans for 2 to 3 minutes. Transfer to wire racks to cool completely. Yield: 4 dozen cookies

COCONUT BUTTERBALLS

1 cup butter, softened (no substitutions)
½ cup powdered sugar
2 cups flour
1½ cups sweetened, flaked coconut, coarsely chopped
Additional powdered sugar

In a large bowl, cream butter and powdered sugar. Gradually blend in flour. Fold in coconut. Roll dough into 1-inch balls. Roll in powdered sugar and place 1 inch apart on ungreased cookie sheets. Bake at 350 degrees for 18 to 20 minutes, until lightly browned. Roll in powdered sugar again while still warm and cool on wire racks. Yield: 4 dozen cookies

SOUTHERN PRALINE COOKIES

2 cups butter
2 cups powdered sugar
4 cups sifted flour
2 cups pecans, chopped
2 tablespoons vanilla

Praline Sauce:
½ cup butter
1 cup light brown sugar
Dash salt
½ cup evaporated milk
2 cups powdered sugar

Cream butter. Add powdered sugar and beat together. Add flour slowly; mix well. Stir in pecans and vanilla. Shape into 1-inch balls and place on ungreased cookie sheet. Use finger to make an indention in each dough ball. Bake at 375 degrees for 12 to 14 minutes. While cookies bake, prepare praline sauce: Melt butter in saucepan and add remaining ingredients. Bring to a boil. Remove from heat and cool. Spoon small amount of praline sauce onto each warm cookie.

LEMON SNOWFLAKE COOKIES

1 box lemon cake mix with pudding
1 egg
2¼ cups frozen whipped topping, thawed
2 cups powdered sugar

Mix cake mix, egg, and whipped topping together. Beat with electric mixer on medium speed until well blended and sticky. Drop batter by teaspoonfuls into powdered sugar and roll to coat. Place cookies on ungreased baking sheets. Bake at 350 degrees for 8 to 10 minutes or until lightly browned.

OATMEAL DROP COOKIES

2 cups flour, sifted
1½ cups sugar
1 teaspoon baking powder
½ teaspoon baking soda
½ teaspoon salt
1 teaspoon cinnamon
3 cups rolled oats

1 cup raisins
¾ to 1 cup semisweet chocolate chips (optional)
1 cup oil
2 eggs
½ cup milk

Sift together flour, sugar, baking powder, baking soda, salt, and cinnamon. Mix in oats, raisins, and chocolate chips (if desired). Add oil, eggs, and milk. Mix until thoroughly blended. Drop by teaspoonfuls onto ungreased cookie sheets. Bake at 375 degrees for 10 minutes. Yield: about 6 dozen

ORANGE-CRANBERRY DROPS

½ cup sugar
½ cup brown sugar, packed
¼ cup butter, softened
1 egg
3 tablespoons orange juice
½ teaspoon orange extract

1 teaspoon orange zest
1½ cups flour
½ teaspoon baking powder
¼ teaspoon baking soda
¼ teaspoon salt
1 cup dried cranberries

Cream together sugars and butter. Stir in egg, orange juice, orange extract, and orange zest. Sift together flour, baking powder, baking soda, and salt. Stir dry ingredients into orange mixture. Fold in dried cranberries. Drop by heaping teaspoonfuls 2 inches apart onto greased cookie sheets. Bake at 375 degrees for 10 to 12 minutes or until edges begin to brown. Cool on baking sheets or remove to cool on wire racks.

RICH WINTER WONDERLAND SQUARES

½ cup margarine,
1 cup graham cracker crumbs
1 cup sweetened, flaked coconut
1 can sweetened condensed milk
1 cup chocolate chips
1 cup butterscotch chips
1 cup pecans (or any nuts)

Place margarine in 9x13-inch cake pan and melt in warm oven. Add all ingredients in the order listed, layering them in the pan. Bake at 350 degrees for about 20 minutes or until mixture pulls away from sides of pan. Allow time to cool before cutting into 18 to 24 squares.

CRANBERRY-PECAN BARS

1 cup flour
2 tablespoons sugar
⅓ cup butter or margarine, softened
1 cup finely chopped pecans, divided
1¼ cups sugar
2 tablespoons flour
2 eggs, beaten
2 tablespoons milk
1 tablespoon orange zest
1 teaspoon vanilla
1 cup cranberries, chopped
½ cup sweetened, flaked coconut

In a medium mixing bowl, combine 1 cup flour and 2 tablespoons sugar. With a pastry blender, cut ⅓ cup butter into flour mixture until mixture resembles coarse crumbs. Stir in ½ cup pecans. Press flour mixture into the bottom of an ungreased 9x13-inch baking pan. Bake at 350 degrees for 15 minutes. Meanwhile, combine 1¼ cups sugar and 2 tablespoons flour. Add eggs, milk, orange zest, and vanilla. Fold in cranberries, coconut, and remaining chopped pecans. Spread over partially baked crust. Bake for 25 to 30 minutes, until top is golden. Cool completely in pan on a wire rack. Cut into bars while warm. Yield: 3 dozen bars

SCOTTISH SHORTBREAD

1 cup butter, softened (no substitutions)
½ cup plus 2 tablespoons sugar, divided
2 cups sifted flour
¼ teaspoon salt
¼ teaspoon baking powder

Beat butter until light and creamy. Add ½ cup sugar and beat until mixture is fluffy. Sift flour with salt and baking powder; stir into butter mixture. Place dough on an ungreased baking sheet and pat into a ½-inch-thick rectangle. Score dough into 1x2-inch bars with the point of a knife. Sprinkle with remaining sugar and bake in the center of the oven at 350 degrees for 15 minutes, until edges are lightly browned. Cool shortbread on the baking sheet for 15 minutes; cut into bars as marked. Yield: 2 dozen bars

HELLO DOLLYS

½ cup margarine
1 cup graham cracker crumbs
1 cup grated coconut
1 small pkg. butterscotch chips
1 small pkg. chocolate chips
1 can sweetened condensed milk
Pecans, chopped

Melt margarine in a 9x13-inch glass baking dish in a warm oven. In pan, layer in order: graham cracker crumbs, coconut, butterscotch chips, and chocolate chips. Drizzle condensed milk over the top of layers. Then top with a layer of chopped pecans. Bake at 325 degrees 15 to 20 minutes. Cool before cutting into squares.

RITA'S CARROT BARS

4 eggs, room temperature, beaten
2 cups sugar
1½ cup cooking oil
2 teaspoons cinnamon
2 teaspoons baking soda
2 teaspoons salt
3 small jars carrot baby food
2½ cups flour

Cream Cheese Frosting:
1 (8 ounce) package cream cheese,
  softened
½ cup butter softened
1 teaspoon vanilla
3½ to 4 cups powdered sugar

Mix ingredients in order. Grease and flour a jelly roll pan and a 9x13-inch pan. Divide mixture between pans. Bake at 350 degrees for 15 to 20 minutes, until light brown. Let cool. For cream cheese frosting, beat first 3 ingredients well with mixer, adding powdered sugar slowly until mixture reaches desired consistency. Spread frosting evenly over cooled bars.

CRISPY RICE CHRISTMAS TREES

3 tablespoons margarine or butter
1 (10 ounce) bag marshmallows
6 cups crispy rice cereal or chocolate crispy rice cereal

Optional Decorations:
Prepared green frosting or tube icing
Red cinnamon candies
Miniature peppermint candies or crushed pieces of peppermint disc candy
Miniature candy-coated chocolate candies

Melt butter or margarine in large saucepan over low heat. Add marshmallows and stir until melted. Remove from heat. Add cereal. Stir until well coated. Spray 15½x10½x1-inch pan with cooking spray. With waxed paper or a buttered spoon, press the entire mixture evenly into pan. Cool slightly. Using 4-inch Christmas tree cookie cutter, press into mixture and cut out trees. Decorate trees as desired with frosting and candies. Best if served the same day. Store in airtight container for no longer than 2 days.

APRICOT BARS

1½ cups sifted flour
1 teaspoon baking power
½ teaspoon salt
1½ cups rolled oats (not instant)
1 cup brown sugar
¾ cup butter or margarine
¾ cup apricot preserves or jam

Sift together flour, baking powder, and salt; stir in oats and brown sugar. Cut in butter until crumbly. Pat ⅔ of crumb mixture into a lightly greased 9x13-inch baking pan. Spread with preserves. Cover with remaining crumb mixture. Bake in 365-degree oven for 30 to 35 minutes until browned. Cool. Cut into bars.

CARAMEL BARS

1 (14 ounce) bag caramels (44 pieces, unwrapped)
1 (5⅓ ounce) can sweetened condensed milk, divided
1 box German chocolate cake mix
½ cup butter or margarine, melted
1 cup pecans, chopped
1 (6 ounce) package chocolate chips

Melt caramels with ⅓ cup condensed milk. Grease and flour a 9x13-inch baking pan. Mix cake mix, butter, nuts, and remainder of condensed milk. Put half of mixture into pan. Bake 6 minutes at 350 degrees. Sprinkle chocolate chips over hot cake; pour on caramel mixture, and finally top with spoonful dabs of remaining cake mixture. Bake at 350 degrees for 15 minutes. Cool before cutting into bars.

LEMON SQUARES

1 cup flour
½ cup butter or margarine, softened
¼ cup powdered sugar
2 eggs
1 cup sugar
½ teaspoon baking powder
¼ teaspoon salt
2 tablespoons lemon juice

Preheat oven to 350 degrees. Cream flour, butter, and powdered sugar. Press evenly into bottom of ungreased 9x9-inch square pan. Bake 20 minutes. Beat remaining ingredients until light and fluffy, about 3 minutes. Pour over hot crust and bake about 25 minutes longer or until no imprint remains when touched lightly in center. Cool and cut into 2-inch squares. Yield: 16 squares

PECAN PIE BARS

Crust:
1 yellow cake mix, divided
½ cup butter or margarine, softened
1 egg

Filling:
⅔ cup reserved cake mix
1 teaspoon vanilla
½ cup brown sugar
3 eggs
1½ cups dark corn syrup
1 cup pecans, chopped

Generously grease bottom and sides of 9x13-inch baking pan. Reserve ⅔ cup cake mix for filling. In large mixing bowl, combine remaining cake mix, butter, and egg. Mix until crumbly. Press into pan. Bake at 350 degrees for 15 to 20 minutes or until golden. Meanwhile, mix all filling ingredients except pecans. Pour over partially baked crust. Sprinkle with pecans. Return to oven and bake for 30 to 35 minutes more or until filling is set. Cool and cut into bars.

CAKE MIX BROWNIES

1 box German chocolate cake mix
½ cup cooking oil
2 tablespoons water
2 eggs
1 teaspoon vanilla
2 packages chocolate chips
¾ cup nuts, chopped

Mix all ingredients and pour into greased 9x13-inch pan. Bake at 350 degrees for 20 to 30 minutes.

PEPPERMINT STICK BARS

3 cups sugar
1 cup butter or margarine
2 cups milk
3 cups flour
3 teaspoons baking soda
¾ cup baking cocoa
4 medium eggs

Topping:
1⅔ cups white chocolate chips or
    semisweet chocolate chips
4 to 6 peppermint sticks, crushed

Cream sugar and shortening, then add milk, alternating with combined flour, baking soda, and cocoa. Add eggs. Mix well. Spread mixture in greased 9x13-inch baking pan. Bake at 300 degrees for 30 minutes or until done.

Topping: In last 2 minutes of baking time, sprinkle chocolate chips on top of brownies. Spread chocolate and immediately sprinkle crushed peppermint sticks on top.

BUTTERSCOTCH BARS

1 (12 ounce) package butterscotch morsels
½ cup butter or margarine
2 cups graham cracker crumbs
1 cup walnuts, finely chopped
1 (8 ounce) package cream cheese, softened
1 (14 ounce) can sweetened condensed milk
1 egg
1 teaspoon vanilla

Preheat oven to 350 degrees. Grease a 9x13-inch baking dish; set aside. In medium saucepan, melt morsels and butter over low heat, stirring often. Stir in graham cracker crumbs and nuts. Press half of mixture into bottom of pan. In large mixing bowl, with electric mixer on medium, beat cream cheese until fluffy. Beat in condensed milk, egg, and vanilla until smooth. Pour over crumb mixture in pan. Sprinkle remaining crumb mixture on top. Bake 25 to 30 minutes or until toothpick inserted in center comes out clean. Cool completely on wire rack. Refrigerate.

SPICY PUMPKIN BARS

4 large eggs, beaten until frothy
1¾ cups sugar
1 cup cooking oil
2 cups canned pumpkin
2 cups flour

2 teaspoons baking powder
1 teaspoon salt
2 teaspoons pumpkin pie spice
1 cup golden raisins

Add sugar to eggs and beat for 2 minutes. Beat in oil and pumpkin. In separate bowl, sift dry ingredients over raisins; fold dry mixture into egg mixture. Do not overmix. Pour into greased and floured 9x13-inch baking pan. Bake at 350 degrees for 35 to 40 minutes or until done. Cool on wire rack and cut into 24 bars.

FROSTED PEANUT BUTTER BARS

½ cup peanut butter
⅓ cup butter or margarine, softened
1½ cups brown sugar, packed
2 eggs
1 teaspoon vanilla
1½ cups flour
1½ teaspoons baking powder
½ teaspoon salt
¼ cup milk

Frosting:
⅔ cup creamy peanut butter
4 cups powdered sugar
½ cup shortening
⅓ to ½ cup milk

Topping:
½ cup semisweet chocolate chips
1 teaspoon butter or margarine

In a mixing bowl, cream peanut butter, butter, and brown sugar. Beat in eggs and vanilla. Combine flour, baking powder, and salt; gradually add to creamed mixture. Add milk; mix well. Transfer to a greased 15x10-inch baking pan. Bake at 350 degrees for 16 to 20 minutes or until a toothpick inserted near center comes out clean. Cool.

Frosting: In a mixing bowl, cream peanut butter, powdered sugar, and shortening. Gradually beat in enough milk to achieve spreading consistency. Frost cooled bars.

Topping: Melt chocolate chips and butter together to create topping; stir until smooth. Drizzle topping over frosting. Refrigerate.

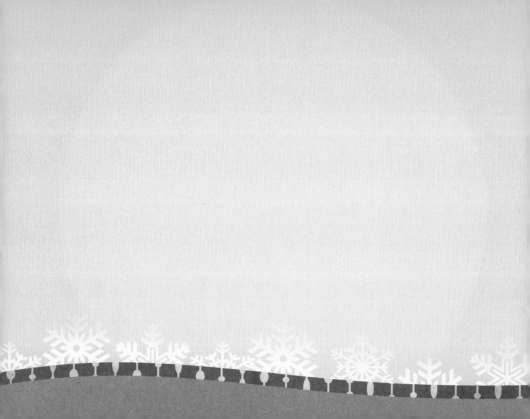

WINTER TEMPTATIONS: YULETIDE CANDIES & FUDGE

Our hearts grow tender with childhood memories and love of kindred,
and we are better throughout the year for having, in spirit,
become a child again at Christmastime.

LAURA INGALLS WILDER

TIGER SWIRL CANDY

1 pound white chocolate
½ cup creamy peanut butter
1 (6 ounce) package semisweet chocolate chips

Melt white chocolate and peanut butter together in microwave on 30-second intervals, stirring each time, just until melted. Melt semisweet chocolate chips in the same manner in another bowl. While chocolate chips are melting, spread peanut butter and white chocolate mixture on a foil-lined 11x15-inch cookie sheet. Drizzle melted chocolate chips over peanut butter mixture, and swirl together with a spoon to create marble effect. Chill thoroughly, and break into pieces. Keep candy refrigerated. Yield: approximately 1½ pounds of candy

ENGLISH TOFFEE

1 cup sliced almonds, toasted
1 cup butter
1 cup sugar
3 tablespoons water
1 tablespoon light corn syrup
Milk chocolate chips

Spread almonds evenly on greased cookie sheet. Melt butter over medium heat. Add sugar and stir until dissolved. Add water and corn syrup. Cook, stirring occasionally, until temperature on candy thermometer reaches about 300 degrees. Pour mixture over almonds on cookie sheet. Sprinkle chocolate chips on top and let sit for a few minutes while chips melt. Spread melted chocolate chips evenly over almond mixture, and sprinkle finely chopped almonds on top. Chill, and then break into small pieces.

CHOCOLATE PRALINE BARS

Graham crackers
1 cup butter or margarine
1 cup light brown sugar
1 cup pecans, chopped
6 (1.5 ounce) plain chocolate bars

Line a 9x9-inch square pan with graham crackers. In a medium saucepan, melt butter and add brown sugar and pecans. Bring to a boil for approximately 3 minutes. Pour mixture over graham crackers. Bake at 350 degrees for 8 minutes. Remove from oven. Immediately place a layer of chocolate bars on top. Wait about 2 minutes and spread evenly with knife when chocolate softens. Chill until chocolate hardens. Cut into bars. Yield: 20 bars

DIVINE DIVINITY

2⅔ cups sugar
⅔ cup light corn syrup
½ cup water
2 egg whites
1 teaspoon vanilla
⅔ cups broken nuts

Stir sugar, corn syrup, and water over low heat until sugar is dissolved. Cook, without stirring, to 260 degrees on candy thermometer. In mixing bowl, beat egg whites until stiff peaks form. Continue beating while pouring hot syrup in a thin stream into egg whites. Add vanilla; beat until mixture holds its shape and becomes slightly dull. Mixture may become too stiff for mixer. Fold in nuts. Drop mixture from tip of buttered spoon onto waxed paper. This recipe works best if not prepared on a humid day. Yield: 4 dozen candies

CHRISTMAS POPCORN BALLS

3 quarts unbuttered popcorn, popped
½ pound candied cherries, cut into small pieces
2 cups light corn syrup
1 tablespoon white vinegar
1 teaspoon salt
2 teaspoons vanilla

In a large bowl, combine popped popcorn and candied cherries. In a 2-quart kettle, combine corn syrup, vinegar, salt; cook, stirring occasionally until candy thermometer reads 250 degrees. Blend vanilla into mixture. Slowly pour corn syrup mixture over popcorn and candied cherries until coated. Quickly and gently shape into 3-inch balls. Yield: approximately 15 popcorn balls.

JULIE'S PEANUT BUTTER BALLS

1½ cups graham cracker crumbs
1½ cups peanut butter
1 (16 ounce) box powdered sugar
¾ cups butter, melted
2 cups semisweet chocolate chips or baking chocolate squares
¼ block paraffin

Combine graham cracker crumbs, peanut butter, powdered sugar, and butter with mixer until blended. Form into ½-inch balls. Place balls on waxed paper and chill in freezer 1 hour. Melt chocolate and paraffin. Dip balls in chocolate. Place on waxed paper to set.

PULLED MOLASSES TAFFY

2 cups light molasses
2 teaspoons white vinegar
1½ tablespoons butter or margarine
½ teaspoon salt
½ teaspoon baking soda

In 3-quart kettle, mix molasses and vinegar. Cook gently, stirring until mixture reaches 260 degrees on candy thermometer. Remove from heat. Add butter, salt, and baking soda. Stir until foaming stops. Pour into greased 9x13-inch glass pan.

When candy is cool enough to pull, lift corners, draw to center, and press together. Pull, using thumbs and fingers, and fold. Repeat until light in color and slightly firm. Pull into two long ropes, ¾ inch thick. Twist. Two people are required for these two steps. With scissors (dipped often into hot water), cut into 1-inch pieces. Wrap in waxed paper. Yield: About 6½ dozen pieces

SOFT PEANUT BUTTER PEANUT BRITTLE

2 cups sugar
¼ cup water
1½ cups light corn syrup
2 cups salted peanuts
2 to 2½ cups peanut butter
½ teaspoon vanilla
1½ teaspoons baking soda

Combine sugar and water in heavy saucepan. Bring mixture to full rolling boil over high heat, stirring constantly. Stir in corn syrup. Cook to hard-crack stage, 300 degrees. Meanwhile, mix peanuts, peanut butter, and vanilla. Remove syrup from heat; at once add peanut butter mixture and baking soda; stir. Working quickly, pour onto buttered cookie sheet; spread with fork. Cool; break into pieces.

MICROWAVE PEANUT BRITTLE

1 cup raw peanuts
1 cup sugar
½ cup light corn syrup
⅛ teaspoon salt
1 teaspoon butter
1 teaspoon vanilla
½ teaspoon baking soda

Mix peanuts, sugar, syrup, and salt in a 1½-quart glass casserole dish. Microwave on high for 8 minutes, stirring after 4 minutes. Stir in butter and vanilla, then cook for 2 more minutes. Stir in baking soda. Pour onto a greased baking sheet. Using two forks, stretch until thin. Cool, then break into pieces.

CINNAMON CANDIED APPLES

12 craft popsicle sticks
12 apples
1⅔ cups cinnamon red hot candies
2 tablespoons water

Insert sticks into apples. Line a baking sheet with waxed paper. Pour candies and water in a heavy-bottomed saucepan over medium-high heat. Occasionally brushing down sides of pan with a heat-resistant pastry brush, heat candy to 300 to 310 degrees. Remove from heat and let cool slightly. Dip apples into hot liquid and place on waxed paper to harden.

CHRISTMAS CRUNCH

2 cups sugar
⅔ cup light corn syrup
½ cup water
3 tablespoons butter
1 teaspoon vanilla
½ teaspoon baking soda
2 cups crispy rice cereal
1 cup cashews

Grease a 10x15-inch baking pan. In a large saucepan over medium heat, combine sugar, corn syrup, and water; bring to a boil, stirring constantly until sugar is dissolved. Continue to cook, without stirring, until candy thermometer reads 300 degrees. Remove from heat; stir in butter, vanilla, and baking soda. Add cereal and cashews; pour into prepared pan to cool thoroughly. Break into pieces and store in airtight container.

CHRISTMAS TURTLE CANDIES

4 ounces pecan halves
24 caramels
1 cup semisweet chocolate chips
1 teaspoon butter or margarine

Preheat oven to 300 degrees. Cover cookie sheet with aluminum foil, shiny side up. Lightly grease foil with nonstick spray. Place 3 pecan halves in a Y shape on foil. Place 1 caramel candy on center of each Y. Repeat. Bake just until caramel is melted, about 9 to 10 minutes. Heat chocolate chips and butter over low heat just until chocolate is melted. Spread over candies and refrigerate for 30 minutes.

WHITE CHOCOLATE-COVERED PRETZELS

6 (1 ounce) squares white chocolate
1 (15 ounce) package mini twist pretzels
¼ cup red and green candy sprinkles

Melt white chocolate in double boiler, stirring constantly. Dip pretzel halfway into white chocolate, completely covering half of the pretzel. Roll in sprinkles if desired, and lay on waxed paper. Continue process until you have desired number of dipped pretzels. Place in refrigerator for 15 minutes to harden. Store in airtight container.

GINA'S FAVORITE FUDGE

3 cups sugar
¾ cup butter
⅔ cup evaporated milk
1 (12 ounce) package semisweet chocolate chips
1 (7 ounce) jar marshmallow crème
1 teaspoon vanilla
1 cup chopped pecans (or walnuts)

Combine sugar, butter, and evaporated milk in heavy 2½-quart saucepan. Bring to a full rolling boil, stirring constantly. Continue to boil 5 minutes over medium heat, stirring constantly to prevent scorching. Remove from heat; add chocolate chips and stir until melted. Add marshmallow crème, vanilla, and nuts; beat until well blended. Pour into greased 9x13-inch pan. Place in refrigerator for approximately 1 to 2 hours, until solid enough to cut into squares.

LAYERED FUDGE

2 pounds powdered sugar, divided
½ cup baking cocoa
1 cup margarine, divided
½ cup milk, divided

Pecans (optional)
2 teaspoons vanilla, divided
½ cup peanut butter

Chocolate layer: Mix 1 pound powdered sugar, cocoa, ½ cup margarine, ¼ cup milk, and pecans (optional) in 1½-quart microwave-safe baking dish. Microwave approximately 2½ minutes, until margarine melts. Add 1 teaspoon vanilla and stir well. Spread mixture in 8x12-inch glass baking dish.

Peanut butter layer: Mix 1 pound powdered sugar, ½ cup peanut butter, ½ cup margarine, and ¼ cup milk in 1½-quart microwave safe baking dish. Microwave for approximately 2½ minutes, until margarine melts. Add 1 teaspoon vanilla and stir well. Spread peanut butter mixture on top of chocolate layer. Refrigerate 1 hour before cutting into squares and serving.

LEIGH'S PEPPERMINT FUDGE

2 tablespoons margarine, divided
2 cups semisweet chocolate chips
1 tub chocolate fudge frosting
1 tub vanilla or white frosting

2 cups white chocolate chips
½ cup crushed peppermints
2 drops red food coloring
1 package chocolate after-dinner mints

Line 9x13-inch pan with aluminum foil, extending it over edges of pan. Grease foil lightly. In saucepan, combine 1 tablespoon margarine and semisweet chocolate chips, stirring over low heat until mixture becomes smooth. Remove from heat and add chocolate fudge frosting. Spread mixture in foiled pan and refrigerate for 20 minutes. In saucepan, combine 1 tablespoon margarine and white chocolate chips, stirring over low heat until mixture becomes smooth. Remove from heat and add vanilla or white frosting, crushed peppermints, and red food coloring. When combined, spread this mixture onto the hardened chocolate layer in the foiled pan. Cut after-dinner mints into fourths, and place in rows across the top of fudge. Let fudge harden in refrigerator. Cut into 1-inch squares.

PEANUT BUTTER FUDGE

2 cups sugar
½ cup milk
1½ cups peanut butter
1 (7 ounce) jar marshmallow crème

In a saucepan, bring sugar and milk to a boil. Boil 3 minutes. Add peanut butter and marshmallow crème; mix well and quickly. Immediately pour into a buttered pan. Size of pan depends on how thick you like your fudge. Chill until set. Cut into squares.

PARTY PERFECTION: CHRISTMAS PUDDINGS, PIES, & PASTRIES

It is good to be children sometimes, and never better than at Christmas, when its mighty founder was a child himself.

CHARLES DICKENS

STOVETOP BREAD PUDDING

½ cup butter
1 cup brown sugar, firmly packed
¼ cup raisins, optional
6 to 7 slices quality bread
  (recommended: day-old French bread
  with crusts)
Butter

2 eggs
1 cup warm milk, scalded
½ cup sugar
Pinch salt
1 teaspoon vanilla
Whipped cream and/or ice cream
  (optional)

Place butter in double boiler and sprinkle brown sugar on top along with raisins. Butter bread slices (trim crusts if desired), and cut into cubes. Put bread cubes on top of brown sugar and butter. Mix eggs, scalded milk, sugar, salt, and vanilla. Pour this mixture over bread cubes. Cover; place over simmering water; steam for 1½ hours. Do not lift lid or stir. Be careful to watch water level in bottom of double boiler. Serve warm in glass dishes or stem glasses. Ladle caramel sauce that forms under the pudding over each serving. Serve with a dollop of whipped cream or ice cream if desired. Yield: 6 servings

PUDDING DELIGHT

2 small boxes vanilla instant pudding mix
1 cup powdered sugar
1 box graham crackers
1 (9 ounce) container whipped dessert topping
1 tub prepared chocolate icing

Beat pudding, powdered sugar, and milk until smooth. Add whipped dessert topping.
Place layer of graham crackers in bottom of pan. Cover with half of the pudding. Add
more crackers, followed by remainder of pudding. Top with more crackers and icing.
Refrigerate overnight.

MALOY'S FANTASTIC DESSERT

Crust:
½ cup butter
¼ cup powdered sugar
1 cup flour
½ cup pecans, chopped

First Layer:
8 ounces cream cheese,
   room temperature
1 cup whipped dessert
   topping
1 cup powdered sugar

Second Layer:
1 large package chocolate
   instant pudding mix
1¾ cups milk
2 cups whipped dessert
   topping
¼ cup pecans, finely
   chopped

Crust: Melt butter. Mix sugar, flour, and pecans into the butter. Spread it in a 9x13-inch dish for your crust. Bake at 375 degress for 15 minutes or until lightly brown.

First Layer: Mix all ingredients well, avoiding clumps. Spread onto cooled crust.

Second Layer: Beat together pudding mix and milk until thick, then spread over second layer. Top with a thin layer of whipped cream and garnish with finely chopped pecans.

DEATH BY CHOCOLATE

1 (9 ounce) box chocolate mousse mix, prepared
1 teaspoon vanilla
¼ cup sugar
2 cups whipping cream
1 pan brownies, homemade or bakery purchased, cut into bite-size squares
3 toffee chocolate candy bars, crushed

Prepare chocolate mousse according to the box directions and refrigerate. Add vanilla and sugar to whipping cream and whip. Using ½ of each ingredient at a time, assemble this layered dessert in a trifle or fruit bowl. Layer in the following order: brownies, mousse, whipped cream mixture, candy bar pieces. Repeat layers. Refrigerate. Yield: 10 to 12 servings

SHIRLEY'S FRUIT TRIFLE

1 angel food cake
1 can peach pie filling
1 large can pineapple chunks, drained
1 large package vanilla instant pudding, prepared
1 large container whipped topping
1 pint fresh strawberries, washed, dried, and sliced
3 bananas, sliced and dipped in lemon juice or fruit preservative

Cover the bottom of trifle bowl or punch bowl with medium-size chunks of cake. Spread a layer of pudding on top, followed by layer of peach pie filling. Add a layer of whipped topping. Then add a layer each of strawberries, pineapples, and bananas. Repeat the process until all ingredients are used. Trifle is pretty with whipped topping and sliced strawberries on top.

EASY PECAN PIE

1 (9-inch) unbaked pie shell
¾ cups sugar
1¼ cups light corn syrup
1 teaspoon vanilla
4 eggs
¼ cup butter
1 cup pecans

Mix above ingredients and pour into unbaked pie shell. Bake 10 minutes at 450 degrees. Then turn oven down to 350 degrees and bake 40 additional minutes.

CREAMY PUMPKIN PIE

1 (9 inch) unbaked pie shell
2 cups canned pumpkin
2/3 cup firmly packed brown sugar
1/2 teaspoon ginger
1/2 teaspoon nutmeg

1 teaspoon cinnamon
1/8 teaspoon ground cloves
1/2 teaspoon salt
2 eggs, slightly beaten
1 cup cream

Bake pie shell at 450 degrees for 10 minutes. Combine pumpkin, brown sugar, ginger, nutmeg, cinnamon, cloves, and salt. In seperate bowl, combine eggs and cream. Add eggs and cream to pumpkin mixture, mixing well until smooth. Fill pie shell with mixture. Bake at 350 degrees for 50 to 60 minutes or until pie tests done. Serve with whipped cream if desired.

APPLE CRUMBLE PIE

1 (9 inch) deep-dish pie shell, unbaked
5 cups peeled, thinly sliced apples (about 5 medium)
½ cup sugar
¾ teaspoon ground cinnamon
⅓ cup sugar
¾ cup flour
6 tablespoons butter

Arrange apple slices in unbaked pie shell. Mix ½ cup sugar with cinnamon; sprinkle over apples. Mix ⅓ cup sugar with flour; cut in butter until crumbly. Spoon mixture over apples. Bake at 400 degrees for 35 to 40 minutes or until apples are soft and top is lightly browned. Yield: 8 servings

CHOCOLATE PECAN PIE

1½ cups pecans, coarsely chopped
1 cup semisweet chocolate chips
1 (8-inch) pie shell, partially baked
½ cup light corn syrup
½ cup sugar
2 eggs, lightly beaten
¼ cup butter, melted

Sprinkle pecans and chocolate chips into pie shell. In a bowl, combine corn syrup, sugar, eggs, and butter. Mix well. Slowly pour mixture over pecans and chocolate. Bake at 325 degrees for 1 hour. Yield: 8 to 12 servings

CARAMEL APPLE PIE

6 cups peeled, thinly sliced tart apples (about 6 medium)
¾ cup sugar
¼ cup flour
¼ teaspoon salt
Pastry for double-crust pie, unbaked
2 tablespoons butter or margarine, melted
⅓ cup caramel ice cream topping
4 tablespoons pecans, chopped

In a large bowl, combine apples, sugar, flour, and salt. Spoon apple mixture into pastry-lined pie pan. Dot with butter. Top with second pastry. Flute edges and cut slits in several places to let steam escape. Bake at 425 degrees for 35 to 45 minutes or until apples are tender. Cover edge of piecrust with strip of foil during last 10 to 15 minutes of baking to prevent excessive browning. Remove pie from oven and immediately drizzle with caramel topping and sprinkle with pecans. Yield: 8 servings

BUTTERSCOTCH PIE

1 (9-inch) pie shell, baked
1½ cups brown sugar
¼ teaspoon salt
2 tablespoons flour
3 tablespoons cornstarch
1½ cups hot water
2 egg yolks
1 tablespoon butter
1 teaspoon vanilla

Meringue:
2 egg whites
¼ teaspoon cream of tartar
½ teaspoon vanilla
4 tablespoons sugar

In a medium saucepan, mix together sugar, salt, flour, and cornstarch. Stir in hot water, blending well. Cook until thick and clear. Beat egg yolks. Add a small amount of hot mixture to egg yolks and mix well. Slowly blend egg yolks into hot sugar mixture, stirring constantly. Cook, stirring constantly, over low heat for 1 minute. Remove from heat and stir in butter and vanilla. Cool slightly, then pour into baked pie shell. Prepare meringue.

Meringue: Beat egg whites with cream of tartar and vanilla until soft peaks form. Add in sugar one tablespoon at a time, beating until stiff peaks form and sugar is dissolved. Spread meringue evenly over pie, sealing at pastry edges. Bake at 350 degrees for 12 to 15 minutes or until meringue is golden. Let cool before serving. Yield: 8 servings

CARAMEL PIE

2 (14 ounce) cans sweetened condensed milk
1 (9-inch) prepared shortbread crust
1 (12 ounce) carton frozen whipped topping, thawed

Remove labels from condensed milk cans. Place in a large pot and cover completely with water. Bring water to a boil over high heat; reduce heat to medium-high for 4 hours, adding water to keep cans covered. Remove cans from pot and cool slightly. Very carefully open cans and pour cooked milk into shortbread crust. Chill. Prior to serving, spread whipped topping evenly over pie. Yield: 8 to 12 servings

FRESH FRUIT COBBLER

4 cups fresh fruit of choice
2 tablespoons butter
¾ cups sugar

Crust:
½ cup butter or margarine
1 cup flour
½ cup sugar
1½ teaspoons baking powder
Salt
½ cup milk

Put first 3 ingredients into pot on stove, cover with water, and bring to a boil. Pour this fruit mixture into baking dish. Mix crust ingredients together and pour batter over fruit mixture. Bake at 400 degrees for 25 minutes.

Note:
For peaches: sprinkle with nutmeg.
For blueberries: add ½ to 1 teaspoon vanilla.

FRENCH SILK PIE

1 (9-inch) pie shell, baked
1 cup sugar
¾ cup butter (no substitutions)
3 (1 ounce) squares unsweetened chocolate, melted and cooled
1½ teaspoons vanilla
¾ cup egg substitute

In a mixing bowl, cream together sugar and butter until light and fluffy. Blend in chocolate and vanilla. Slowly add egg substitute, ¼ cup at a time, beating 2 to 3 minutes after each addition and scraping sides of bowl frequently. Pour into baked pie shell and chill thoroughly. Yield: 6 to 8 servings

FUDGE NUT BROWNIE PIE

1 (9-inch) pie shell, unbaked
1 (14 ounce) can sweetened condensed milk
½ cup baking cocoa
¼ cup butter or margarine
1 cup flour
3 large eggs, beaten
1 teaspoon vanilla
1¾ cups pecans, chopped

In a medium saucepan over low heat, stir together milk, cocoa, and butter. When butter melts and mixture is heated through, remove from heat. Stir in flour, eggs, vanilla, and pecans; pour into pie shell. Bake at 350 degrees for 50 minutes or until center is set. Yield: 8 servings

PEANUT BUTTER PIE

1 (8 ounce) package cream cheese, softened
⅔ cup creamy peanut butter
1 (14 ounce) can sweetened condensed milk
1 (8 ounce) carton frozen whipped topping, thawed
1 prepared graham cracker crumb crust

Beat cream cheese, peanut butter, and condensed milk together until smooth. Fold in whipped topping. Spoon into graham cracker crust. Chill. Yield: 8 servings

QUICK CHOCOLATE BAR PIE

1 (7 ounce) milk chocolate bar, divided
2 tablespoons milk
1 (8 ounce) carton frozen whipped topping, thawed and divided
1 (9-inch) pie shell, baked

Melt chocolate bar, minus 3 squares, in a pot placed over hot (not boiling) water. Gradually stir in milk. Cool slightly, then fold in whipped topping. Blend well; pour into prepared pie shell. Grate or shave remaining chocolate over pie. Chill. Yield: 8 servings

CLASSIC CHESS PIE

2 eggs, beaten
1½ cups sugar
1 tablespoon flour
1 tablespoon white cornmeal
¼ cup milk
½ cup butter, melted
½ teaspoon vanilla
½ teaspoon white vinegar
1 (9-inch) pie shell, unbaked

In a mixing bowl, combine eggs with sugar, flour, and cornmeal. Add in milk, butter, vanilla, and vinegar. Pour into unbaked pie shell. Bake at 325 degrees for 45 minutes. Decrease oven temperature to 300 degrees and bake an additional 10 minutes. Yield: 8 servings

INDIVIDUAL CHRISTMAS CHEESECAKES

3 (8 ounce) packages cream cheese
2½ teaspoons vanilla, divided
1¼ cups sugar, divided
5 eggs
2 cups sour cream
Red and green candied cherries

Line 1½-inch muffin tins with paper liners. Set aside. Mix cream cheese with 1½ teaspoons vanilla. Add 1 cup sugar and eggs; beat well. Spoon 1 tablespoon mixture into each paper cup. Bake at 350 degrees for about 20 minutes or until top cracks slightly. For topping, combine sour cream, remaining ¼ cup sugar, and remaining 1 teaspoon vanilla; mix well. Spoon small amount of topping onto each cooked cheesecake. Return to oven, and bake 5 minutes. Cool on racks. Decorate with cherries. Refrigerate until ready to serve cakes. Yield: 2 dozen individual cakes

COCONUT CREAM PIE

1 (9-inch) pie shell, baked
⅔ cup sugar
¼ cup cornstarch
½ teaspoon salt
3 cups milk
4 egg yolks, lightly beaten
2 tablespoons butter
2 teaspoons vanilla
¾ cup sweetened, flaked coconut

Whipped Cream Topping:
1 cup heavy cream, chilled
1 teaspoon powdered sugar
¼ cup sweetened, flaked coconut, toasted

In a saucepan, mix sugar, cornstarch, and salt. Blend together milk and egg yolks and gradually stir into sugar mixture. Cook over medium heat, stirring constantly, until mixture is thickened and bubbly. Cook for 1 minute, stirring constantly; remove from heat. Stir in butter, vanilla, and coconut. Let cool slightly. Pour into baked pie shell and cover with plastic wrap. Chill pie thoroughly for at least 2 hours. Prepare and cover with whipped cream topping.

Whipped Cream Topping: Whip cream together with powdered sugar until stiff peaks form. Spread evenly over pie and sprinkle with toasted coconut. Yield: 8 servings

CAROL'S CHERRY CHEESECAKE TARTS

2 (8 ounce) packages cream cheese
½ cup sugar
1 teaspoon vanilla
2 eggs
1 tablespoon lemon juice
Vanilla wafers
1 can cherry pie filling

Mix cream cheese, sugar, vanilla, eggs, and lemon juice well until blended and creamy. Place vanilla wafers (flat side down) in paper cupcake liners set in a muffin tin. Spoon about 2 tablespoons filling on top of each wafer. Bake 20 minutes at 350 degrees or until slightly cracked on top. Cool. Top each tart with cherry pie filling, including about three cherries per tart. Refrigerate. Serve cool.

A SLICE OF THE HOLIDAYS: CHRISTMAS CAKES

It comes every year and will go on forever. And along with Christmas belong the keepsakes and the customs. Those humble, everyday things a mother clings to, and ponders, like Mary, in the secret spaces of her heart.

MARJORIE HOLMES

CRANBERRY BUNDT CAKE

2 cups flour
1 teaspoon baking powder
¾ teaspoon baking soda
½ teaspoon salt
⅔ cup butter or margarine, softened
1 cup sugar

3 eggs
1½ teaspoons vanilla
1 (8 ounce) package sour cream
¾ cup dried cranberries, chopped
⅓ cup pecans, chopped
Powdered sugar

In a small bowl, combine flour, baking powder, baking soda, and salt. Set aside. In a mixing bowl, cream butter with sugar. Add eggs one at a time, beating well after each addition. Stir in vanilla. Add dry ingredients to creamed mixture alternately with sour cream. Stir in cranberries and pecans and pour into greased and floured 8-inch Bundt cake pan. Bake at 350 degrees for 45 to 50 minutes or until a wooden pick inserted in cake comes out clean. Cool 10 minutes before removing from pan. Dust with powdered sugar. Yield: 8 to 10 servings

TOFFEE COFFEE CAKE

2 cups brown sugar, packed
2 cups flour, sifted
1 cup butter or margarine
1 large egg, beaten
1 cup buttermilk

1 teaspoon vanilla
1 teaspoon baking soda
⅛ teaspoon salt
8 ounces toffee candy, crushed
½ cup pecans, chopped

In a medium bowl, combine brown sugar, flour, and butter to form a crumbly mixture. Reserve 1 cup for topping. In another bowl, combine egg, buttermilk, vanilla, baking soda, and salt. Add to first mixture; blend well with an electric mixer. Spoon into a greased 9x13-inch pan. Sprinkle with reserved topping, crushed toffee candy, and chopped pecans. Bake at 350 degrees for 50 to 55 minutes. Yield: 16 servings

COCONUT CHRISTMAS CAKE

¾ cup butter or margarine, softened
1½ cups sugar
3 eggs
1 cup milk
¾ teaspoon coconut flavoring
¾ teaspoon salt
3 cups flour
3 teaspoons baking powder

Cake Glaze:
½ cup water
1 tablespoon sugar

Coconut Frosting:
2 cups whipping cream
½ cup sugar
1 teaspoon vanilla
1 teaspoon lemon extract
2 drops butter flavoring

Cake Garnish:
3 cups canned coconut (grated)
Candied cherries

Cream butter; add 1½ cups sugar gradually, beating well. Add eggs, one at a time; beat well. Mix coconut flavoring into milk. Add sifted dry ingredients to butter mixture alternately with milk/flavoring mixture. Grease and lightly flour three 8-inch round cake pans. Pour batter into pans. Bake at 350 degrees for 25 to 30 minutes until a toothpick inserted in center comes out clean. Cool cake in pans on wire racks for 10 minutes; remove from pans and cool cake layers completely on wire racks.

Cake Glaze: Combine ½ cup water and 1 tablespoon sugar in a small saucepan; bring to a boil. Lower heat and simmer 3 minutes, stirring. Then drizzle glaze over all 3 cake layers to prepare for frosting.

Coconut Frosting: Mix all ingredients well. Frost tops of first 2 layers and cover each frosted layer with ½ cup coconut. Stack these two layers on a cake plate. Add top layer; cover top and sides of cake with frosting.

Cake Garnish: Cover top and sides of cake with remaining coconut. For a final festive touch, decorate top of cake with candied cherries. Chill in refrigerator until ready to serve.

ORANGE AND PINEAPPLE CAKE DELIGHT

1 box butter cake mix
½ cup cooking oil
4 eggs
1 small can mandarin oranges (undrained)
1 large can crushed pineapple (undrained)
1 (3¾ ounce) box vanilla instant pudding mix
1 large container whipped dessert topping

Place cake mix, oil, eggs, and oranges into a bowl and beat. Pour into 3 greased 9-inch cake pans. Bake at 325 degrees for 30 minutes. Cool to room temperature. Place pineapple in a bowl. Sprinkle pudding over it and fold in whipped dessert topping. Ice cake with this mixture and place in refrigerator. Serve chilled.

DUMP CAKE

1 (20 ounce) can crushed pineapple (undrained)
1 (21 ounce) can cherry pie filling
1 box yellow cake mix
1 cup butter or margarine, cut into thin slices
¼ cup nuts, chopped

Preheat oven to 350 degrees (325 degrees if using glass baking dish). Dump undrained pineapple into baking dish and spread evenly. Dump cherry pie filling evenly on top of the pineapple. Sprinkle the dry cake mix evenly over the pineapple and cherry layers. Place butter slices evenly over top of cake mix. Sprinkle nuts on top. Bake 1 hour. Scoop out with large spoon. Delicious when served warm with a scoop of vanilla ice cream. Dump cake can also be served cool. Yield: 10 to 12 servings

EGGNOG POUND CAKE

1 cup butter, softened
1 cup shortening
3 cups sugar
6 eggs
3 cups flour

1 cup eggnog
1 cup sweetened, flaked coconut
1 teaspoon lemon extract
1 teaspoon vanilla
1 teaspoon coconut extract

Preheat oven to 325 degrees. Cream butter and shortening. Gradually add sugar, beating well. Add eggs, one at a time, beating well. Slowly add flour to creamed mixture alternately with eggnog, beginning and ending with flour. Stir in coconut and lemon, vanilla, and coconut extract flavorings. Pour cake batter into well-greased and floured 10-inch tube pan. Bake at 325 degrees for 1½ hours. Cool 10 minutes before removing from pan.

CREAM CHEESE POUND CAKE

1 (8 ounce) package cream cheese
1½ cups margarine
3 cups sugar
6 large eggs
1 teaspoon vanilla
3 cups cake flour, sifted and then measured

Soften and mix cream cheese and margarine. Stir in sugar until creamed. Add eggs (2 at a time) and vanilla. Blend mixture until smooth. Add cake flour until the mixture has a doughy texture. Put in greased and floured tube or Bundt pan. Bake at 300 degrees for 1½ hours.

RED VELVET CAKE

½ cup shortening
1½ cups sugar
2 eggs
2 tablespoons baking cocoa
1½ ounces red food coloring
2½ cups flour
1 teaspoon salt
1 teaspoon vanilla
1 cup buttermilk
1 teaspoon baking soda
1 tablespoon vinegar

Cream Cheese Frosting:
2 (3 ounce) packages cream cheese,
   softened
1 teaspoon vanilla
6 tablespoons butter, softened
2 cups powdered sugar, sifted

Cream shortening; add sugar gradually. Add eggs, one at a time; beat well. Make paste of cocoa and coloring; add to creamed mixture. Add flour, salt, and vanilla alternately with buttermilk, beating well after each addition. Sprinkle soda over vinegar; pour vinegar over batter. Stir until thoroughly mixed. Bake in three 8-inch-square pans or two 9-inch-square pans for 30 minutes at 350 degrees. Cool before frosting.

Cream Cheese Frosting: Blend all ingredients until smooth. Spread over red velvet cake. Decorate top of cake as desired.

BLACK FOREST CAKE

2 (20 ounce) cans tart pitted cherries, drained, juice reserved
1 cup sugar
¼ cup cornstarch
1½ teaspoons vanilla
2 (9 inch) chocolate cake layers, baked and cooled
3 cups cold whipping cream
⅓ cup powdered sugar

Drain cherries, reserving ½ cup juice. Combine reserved cherry juices, cherries, sugar, and cornstarch in saucepan. Cook and stir over low heat until thickened. Add vanilla; stir. Divide each cake layer in half horizontally. Crumble one half layer; set aside. Beat cold whipping cream and powdered sugar in a large bowl with an electric mixer on high until stiff peaks form. Reserve 1½ cups whipped cream for decorative piping. Place one cake layer on a serving plate. Spread with 1 cup whipped cream; top with ¾ cup cherry topping. Top with second cake layer, 1 cup whipped cream, and ¾ cup cherry topping; top with third cake layer. Frost cake sides with remaining whipped cream; pat gently with reserved cake crumbs. Spoon reserved 1½ cups whipped cream into pastry bag fitted with star tip; pipe around top and bottom edges of cake. Spoon remaining topping over top of cake.

ILA'S SUGARPLUM CAKE

2 cups sugar
2 cups self-rising flour
1 teaspoon cinnamon
1 teaspoon ground cloves
1 cup cooking oil
3 eggs, slightly beaten
2 jars plum (or plum/apple) strained baby food
1 cup nuts, chopped
Powdered sugar

Blend—but do not use mixer—sugar, self-rising flour, cinnamon, and ground cloves. Add oil, eggs, baby food, and nuts. Pour into a greased and floured Bundt cake pan. Bake at 350 degrees for 45 minutes or until a toothpick inserted into the center comes out clean. Cool and invert on cake plate. Dust with sifted powdered sugar.

SOUR CREAM COFFEE CAKE

1 cup pecans, chopped
½ teaspoon cinnamon
1 cup brown sugar
1 cup sour cream
½ teaspoon baking soda
2 eggs, beaten

¾ cups butter or margarine, melted
2 cups flour
2 cups sugar
2 teaspoons baking powder
¼ teaspoon salt
2 cups bread flour, sifted

Combine pecans, cinnamon, and brown sugar, then sprinkle into an 8x10-inch greased pan. In mixing bowl, combine and beat well sour cream, baking soda, eggs, and butter. Resift flour with sugar, baking powder, and salt. Add sifted ingredients to creamed mixture. Beat until smooth. Spread dough over sprinkled mixture. Bake at 350 degrees for 25 minutes.

EARTHQUAKE CAKE

1 small can moist coconut
1 cup pecans or walnuts, chopped
1 box Swiss chocolate cake mix, mixed according to package directions
½ cup butter or margarine, softened
1 (8 ounce) package cream cheese, softened
1 box powdered sugar

Spray a 12x14-inch pan with cooking spray. Mix coconut and nuts together and spread mixture evenly over bottom of pan. Mix cake mix according to directions on box and spread over coconut/nut mixture. Blend together butter, cream cheese, and powdered sugar. Spread this mixture over uncooked cake. Bake in preheated oven for approximately 1 hour.

TURTLE CAKE

1 box German chocolate cake mix
½ cup butter or margarine, softened
1½ cups water
⅓ cup cooking oil
1 can sweetened condensed milk,
    divided
1 pound caramels, unwrapped
Pecans

Frosting:
½ cup butter or margarine
3 tablespoons cocoa
6 tablespoons evaporated milk
1 box powdered sugar
1 teaspoon vanilla

Combine cake mix, butter, water, oil, and half a can of condensed milk. Pour ½ of batter into greased and floured 9x13-inch pan. Bake at 350 degrees for 20 to 25 minutes. Melt and mix caramels with remainder of condensed milk. Spread over baked layer of cake. Sprinkle with chopped pecans. Cover with remaining cake batter. Bake an additional 25 to 35 minutes. Cool. Frost.

Frosting: Melt butter in saucepan with cocoa and milk. Remove from heat and add powdered sugar and vanilla. Blend well.

TEXAS CHOCOLATE SHEET CAKE

1 cup water
4 tablespoons baking cocoa
½ cup butter or margarine
½ cup shortening
2 cups flour
Pinch salt
1½ teaspoons baking soda
¼ teaspoon cinnamon
2 cups sugar
2 eggs
1 teaspoon vanilla
½ cup buttermilk

Icing:
½ cup butter or margarine
4 tablespoons cocoa
6 tablespoons milk
1 box powdered sugar
1 teaspoon vanilla
Pinch salt
1 cup chopped nuts (optional)

Bring water, cocoa, butter, and shortening to a boil. In a separate bowl, mix together flour, salt, baking soda, and cinnamon. Mix in sugar. Add eggs, vanilla, and buttermilk. Add to water mixture and mix well. After combining all ingredients, pour mixture into 9x13-inch baking pan. Bake at 400 degrees for approximately 30 minutes. Cake should be iced immediately after removing from oven.

Icing: Bring to a boil butter, cocoa, and milk. Add powdered sugar, vanilla, salt, and chopped nuts. Stir together.

FAMILY FAVORITE HOT FUDGE SUNDAE CAKE

1 cup flour
¾ cup sugar
2 tablespoons baking cocoa
2 teaspoons baking powder
¼ teaspoon salt
½ cup milk
2 tablespoons cooking oil

1 teaspoon vanilla
1 cup nuts, chopped
1 cup brown sugar, packed
¼ cup baking cocoa
1¾ cups very hot water
Vanilla ice cream

Preheat oven to 350 degrees. Mix flour, sugar, 2 tablespoons cocoa, baking powder, and salt. Mix in milk, oil, and vanilla with fork until smooth. Stir in nuts. Spread in 9x9-inch pan. Sprinkle brown sugar and ¼ cup cocoa over batter. Pour hot water over batter. Bake 40 minutes or until top is dry. Spoon warm cake into dessert dishes. Top with ice cream and spoon some of the sauce onto each serving.

JEWEL CAKES

2 cups pecan pieces
1¾ cups walnut pieces
1¼ cups golden raisins
½ pound pitted dates, chopped
¾ cup red candied cherries, coarsely chopped
¾ cup green candied cherries, coarsely chopped
1½ cups candied pineapple, coarsely chopped
1 (14 ounce) can sweetened condensed milk

In a large mixing bowl, combine all ingredients and mix well with a large spoon. Pack tightly into well-greased mini muffin cups. Bake at 275 degrees for 25 to 30 minutes.
Yield: 24 cakes

CRANBERRY-ORANGE BUNDT CAKE

Cranberry Relish:
1 cup whole cranberry sauce
1 tablespoon grated orange zest
1 tablespoon coarsely walnuts, chopped

Cake:
1 box yellow cake mix
1 (3.5 ounce) box vanilla instant pudding
5 medium eggs
¼ cup orange juice
½ cup milk
½ cup cooking oil

Orange Glaze:
2 tablespoons orange juice
1¼ cups powdered sugar

Cranberry Relish: The day before making the cake, combine cranberry sauce with orange zest. Mix in walnuts. Refrigerate overnight.

Cake: Combine cake ingredients in mixing bowl. Fold in cranberry relish, prepared the day before. Coat Bundt cake pan with nonstick cooking spray. Pour in cake batter. Bake at 350 degrees for 50 to 60 minutes.

Orange Glaze: Whisk together orange juice and powdered sugar. Spread onto cooled cake.

FRESH APPLE CAKE

2 cups sugar
1 cup cooking oil
2 eggs
2 teaspoons vanilla
2 cups flour

1 teaspoon salt
1 teaspoon baking soda
3 cups apples, finely chopped
1 cup pecans, chopped

Cream together sugar and oil. Add remaining ingredients. Pour mixture into greased and floured 10-inch tube pan. Bake at 350 degrees for 45 minutes. Do not open oven door while baking.

PUMPKIN CAKE

3 cups flour
1½ teaspoons salt
½ teaspoon baking powder
1 teaspoon baking soda
1 teaspoon nutmeg
1 teaspoon cinnamon
1 teaspoon allspice
1 cup shortening

2¾ cups sugar
3 eggs
1 teaspoon vanilla
1 (16 ounce) can pumpkin
1 cup pecans, chopped
½ cup powdered sugar
1 tablespoon water

Line bottom of a 10-inch tube pan with waxed paper. Mix flour, salt, baking powder, baking soda, and spices. In seperate bowl, cream shortening; add sugar; add eggs, one at a time. Beat well. Add vanilla. Add dry ingredients and pumpkin. Stir in pecans. Bake in preheated oven at 350 degrees for 1½ hours. While cake is still warm, mix together powdered sugar with water and spread on top, as a glaze.

PUMPKIN DESSERT

4 eggs, slightly beaten
1 (16 ounce) can pumpkin
1 can evaporated milk
1 cup sugar
1 teaspoon salt
½ teaspoon ground cloves
1 teaspoon cinnamon
1 box yellow cake mix
1 cup nuts, chopped
¾ cup butter, melted

Mix together eggs, pumpkin, evaporated milk, sugar, salt, cloves, and cinnamon. Pat this combination into a greased 9x13-inch pan. Sprinkle yellow cake mix and chopped nuts over top. Pour melted butter over all. Bake at 325 degrees for approximately 1½ hours until a knife inserted in center comes out clean.

GRACE BURNHAM'S PINEAPPLE UPSIDE DOWN CAKE

½ cup butter
1 cup brown sugar
1 small can sliced pineapple (drain, reserve juice)
½ cup shredded coconut

1 cup pecans, chopped
1 cup sugar
1 cup flour
3 eggs, separated
4 tablespoons pineapple juice

Place butter in a 9x13-inch pan and melt in warm oven. Sprinkle brown sugar over butter, then place pineapple slices over butter/brown sugar mixture. Spread with coconut and pecans. Set aside.

Combine sugar, flour, egg yolks (save egg whites), and 4 tablespoons pineapple juice in large mixing bowl; blend into a batter. In small mixing bowl, beat egg whites until stiff and fold gently into the batter. Then pour batter on top of the mixture in the baking pan. Bake at 350 degrees for 25 to 30 minutes. Serve warm. Slice and flip each piece of cake upside down so that you serve it pineapple side up.

DECEMBER DELIGHTS: FROZEN HOLIDAY TREATS

For unto us a child is born, unto us a Son is given: and the government shall be upon his shoulder: and his name shall be called Wonderful, Counsellor, The mighty God, the everlasting Father, the Prince of Peace.

ISAIAH 9:6

FROZEN YOGURT BROWNIE PIE (WITH STRAWBERRIES)

¼ cup margarine
⅔ cup brown sugar, firmly packed
½ cup egg substitute
¼ cup buttermilk
¼ cup flour
⅓ cup baking cocoa
¼ teaspoon salt

1 teaspoon vanilla
½ gallon vanilla frozen yogurt, softened
1 quart chocolate non-fat frozen yogurt, softened
¾ cup chocolate syrup
Garnishes: fresh strawberries and/or chocolate curls (optional)

Melt margarine in a large saucepan over medium-high heat. Add brown sugar, stirring with a wire whisk. Remove from heat; cool slightly. Add egg substitute and buttermilk, stirring well. Combine flour, cocoa, and salt; add to buttermilk mixture, stirring until blended. Stir in vanilla. Lightly coat a 9-inch springform pan with nonstick spray. Pour mixture into pan. Bake at 350 degrees for 15 minutes. Cool completely in pan on a wire rack.

When brownie layer is completely cooled, spread half of vanilla yogurt over it; cover and freeze until firm. Spread chocolate yogurt over vanilla yogurt; cover and freeze until firm. Top with remaining vanilla yogurt. Cover and freeze at least 8 hours. Remove sides of pan. Serve each wedge with 1 tablespoon chocolate syrup and desired garnishes. Yield: 12 servings

ICE CREAM PIE

18 chocolate sandwich cookies, crushed
⅓ cup margarine, melted
1 quart ice cream, softened (peppermint, mint chocolate chip, coffee, or other)
1½ semisweet baking chocolate squares
1 tablespoon margarine

½ cup sugar
⅔ cup evaporated milk
4 ounces whipped dessert topping
Nuts, Oreo pieces, crushed peppermint, or other for garnish

Combine crushed cookies with ⅓ cup margarine. Press into 10-inch pie pan or square pan. Spread softened ice cream over crust. Place in freezer. Melt chocolate squares along with 1 tablespoon margarine over low heat. Add sugar and milk. Cook until thick, approximately 10 minutes. Cool thoroughly. Remove pie from freezer once ice cream has hardened and chocolate mixture has cooled. Pour chocolate mixture over pie. Return to freezer. When very firm, spread whipped dessert topping over pie and sprinkle with desired garnish. Freeze until 5 minutes before serving.

FROZEN CHOCOLATE MINT DESSERT

¾ cup crushed vanilla wafers
2 squares unsweetened baking chocolate
⅔ cup butter
2 cups powdered sugar
2 eggs, separated
1 cup pecans, chopped
1 teaspoon vanilla
½ gallon peppermint ice cream (or add crushed peppermint candy to vanilla ice cream)
Chocolate syrup

Cover bottom of ungreased 9x13-inch pan with crushed vanilla wafers. Set aside. Melt chocolate squares and butter over low heat. Stir in powdered sugar, 2 slightly beaten egg yolks, pecans, and vanilla. Fold in stiffly beaten egg whites. Pour over crumbs in pan and chill until firm. When firm, spread softened ice cream on top of first layer. Sprinkle top with additional chopped pecans if desired. Drizzle with chocolate syrup. Cover tightly with foil and freeze.

FROZEN FRUITY DESSERT

¾ cup sugar
½ cup nuts, chopped
1 (8 ounce) package cream cheese
1 (12 ounce) container whipped dessert topping (thawed)
1 small can crushed pineapple, drained
2 bananas, cut in half and sliced
½ bag mini marshmallows
1 (10 ounce) package frozen strawberries, thawed

Mix together. Freeze. Take out about 20 minutes before serving. Serve in spoonfuls.

FROZEN MOCHA CHEESECAKE

1½ cups chocolate wafer cookie crumbs (about 24 cookies)
¼ cup sugar
¼ cup margarine or butter, melted
1 (8 ounce) package cream cheese, softened
1 (14 ounce) can sweetened condensed milk
⅔ cup chocolate syrup
2 tablespoons instant coffee
1 teaspoon hot water
1 cup whipping cream, whipped

In small bowl, combine crumbs, sugar, and margarine. In buttered 9-inch springform pan or 9x13-inch baking dish, pat crumbs firmly on bottom and up sides of pan. Chill. In large mixing bowl, beat cream cheese until fluffy; add sweetened condensed milk and chocolate syrup. In small bowl, dissolve coffee in water; add to the mixture. Mix well. Fold in whipped cream. Pour into prepared pan. Cover. Freeze 6 hours or until firm. Garnish with additional chocolate crumbs if desired. Return leftovers to freezer.

CHILLY LEMON SQUARES

¼ cup margarine, melted
1¼ cups graham cracker crumbs
¼ cup sugar
3 egg yolks
1 (14 ounce) can sweetened condensed milk
½ cup lemon juice
1 (8 ounce) tub whipped dessert topping, thawed

Combine first 3 ingredients and press into 9-inch-square glass baking dish. Beat egg yolks, stir in condensed milk, then lemon juice. Add a few drops of yellow food coloring if desired. Pour into crust; top with 2 cups whipped dessert topping. Cover well and freeze. May serve with an extra dollop of whipped dessert topping if desired. Yield: 9 servings

WHITE CHRISTMAS SNOW ICE CREAM

2 large eggs
½ cup sugar
¼ cup milk
Pinch salt
1 teaspoon vanilla
Fresh snow

Beat eggs well; add sugar and mix well. Add milk, salt, and vanilla. Beat until light and fluffy. Scoop up large amount of snow from a pristine part of yard or patio. Using a large spoon, spoon the snow into the milk mixture slowly. Do not stir! Instead, gently press the snow into the milk mixture to blend. Keep spooning more and more snow into the milk until it begins to become solid and very firm. Serve immediately when ice cream is desired thickness. Do not store leftovers. Yield: 6 to 8 servings

INDEX